Truck Stop

Truck Stop

Photographs by Marc F. Wise

Text by Bryan Di Salvatore

University Press of Mississippi

Jackson

Author and Artist Series

First Edition
Designed by John A. Langston
Printed in Hong Kong

Photographs on preceding pages:
1: Buckhorn, Pennsylvania 1990
2: Bucyrus, Ohio 1990
3: El Paso, Texas 1990
4: Walcott, Iowa 1990

Library of Congress
Cataloging-in-Publication Data

Wise, Marc F.
   Truck stop / photographs by Marc F. Wise,
text by Bryan Di Salvatore.
      p.   cm.
   ISBN 0-87805-838-9 (cloth : alk. paper).
   — ISBN 0-87805-842-7 (limited : alk. paper).
   — ISBN 0-87805-839-7 (paper : alk. paper)
   1. Truck drivers—United States.
2. Truck drivers—United States—Pictorial
works. 3. Trucking—United States.
4. Trucking—United States—Pictorial works.
5. Truck stops—United States. 6. Truck
stops—United States—Pictorial works.
I. Di Salvatore, Bryan. II. Title.
HD8039.M7952U577 1995
388.3'24'0973—dc20   95-14949
                                              CIP
British Library Cataloging-in-Publication data
available

Buda, Texas 1994

Photographer's Preface

My first time going down a mountain, on the way to Spokane with a load of automobile windshields at night, compact snow and ice covering the road, I was going too slow even for an eighteen-wheeler. As I crept through a construction zone, a line of trucks and Christmas travelers backed up the mountain behind me. Someone started to complain on the CB, even after I sheepishly explained that this was my first descent and a dark, wintry one at that. Without hesitation, a second voice, a booming Southern drawl, broke in: "Now, North American, you just keep on doing like you're doing up there. You're doing a *fine* job." And then, knowing another trucker would never hurry a driver down a mountain, he sneered to the complainer, "Where you at, four wheeler? I'll show you how to go down a mountain." I sat there, beaming and breathing a heartfelt sigh of relief. Only another truck driver would show such camaraderie, support, and understanding. Truckers will tell you that you can go down a mountain too slow many times, but you can go down too fast only once.

That first descent was in December of 1987. Only a few months before, I had graduated from the Rhode Island School of Design with a degree in photography. Ten days after graduation, I entered tractor-trailer truck driving school. For a good portion of the next six years, I lived as an over-the-road driver, hauling freight throughout the forty-eight contiguous United States and photographing the world of the long haul truck driver.

I am often asked why a photographer like myself would want to become a truck driver. For me it seemed a perfectly logical thing to do. Growing up in Massachusetts, the son of an economist and a writer, I had always loved our family trips to Washington State, throughout New England, and up to Nova Scotia, and I had travelled a little on my own—to Mexico, to school in Oregon, to Alaska and California, back and forth across the country a couple of times. As I approached graduation, I was full of what I had learned about photography and life. In my own way I wanted to follow in the tracks of photographers I had studied in school—the "gods of photography," we called them: Robert Frank, William Eggleston, Lee Friedlander, Garry Winogrand, Dorothea Lange, Walker Evans, Chauncey Hare, Danny Lyon, Lewis Hine, and others. They now became my mentors and idols. My desire for adventure was influenced by the books of Jack London, Jack Kerouac, Ernest Hemingway, and John Steinbeck. Now I was ready to go out into the world and see what I could do. Commercial photography did not interest me, and I wasn't ready to settle down to a career. Trucking seemed to offer what I was looking for: travel, adventure, challenge, and a means of support. Most importantly, it gave me an opportunity to photograph the life I was living.

So, against the advice of all the truck drivers I shared my plans with, I thrust myself, at the age of twenty-three, into a situation very different from any I had ever known before. In the fall of 1987, I put three hundred dollars down on a 1985 cabover Freightliner and went to work for North American Van Lines out of Fort Wayne, Indiana. My original plan was to transport furniture for families moving across the country and photograph the families at their origin and destination. Soon after I began my job, however, I became captivated by the life of long haul truck drivers and rarely photographed outside that world.

After a year and a half, I sold my truck and took a six-month break. In the fall of 1989 I went to work as a company driver for C.R. England & Sons out of Salt Lake City; for the next six months I drove a conventional Kenworth tractor and pulled a refrigerated van. In 1990 I was honored with a Guggenheim Fellowship and continued my photographic study of truck drivers for four more months. I took another break to pursue other projects but returned to long haul driving in early 1994. For five months I drove a truck for Burlington Motor Carriers out of Monroe, Louisiana, during which time I completed the photography for this book.

All of the truck drivers in these pictures consented to be photographed, and all were told that I was working on a book. I did not pose them except occasionally to ask them to stand by their truck. Usually I just told them to continue doing whatever they were already doing. I used a medium format range finder camera and a hand-held flash.

At first I was unsure of my identity as a truck driver and a photographer, and I was intimidated photographing in and around the truck stops. I worried about how the other drivers would react to me and my camera. I could sense that some drivers were wary of me when they saw my camera equip-

ment, probably assuming I was one of those in the media they had been slandered by on a recent "60 Minutes" program called "Killer Trucks." When they realized that I was a driver, too, they usually dropped their guard and were glad to talk to someone, especially another driver interested in telling the real story of trucking. They would often invite me to sit down with them, buy me a cup of coffee, and tell me about their trucking experiences—about low pay, regulations, and roads in need of repair, about how trucking just isn't the same anymore with computers that monitor where you are and where you need to be and the company always watching you from afar, and about not being able to watch their children grow up day by day. They told me about their grandfathers who drove two-speed, chain-drive Macks in the days before interstate highways, when you had to drive through each city rather than around it. Truck drivers are a proud group. Many I talked to had been driving trucks for more years than I had been alive. I heard about their dreams and goals, their personal philosophies, and their reflections on their lives.

I soon overcame my anxiety. After a few cups of coffee, I would approach the biggest, roughest, most road weary-looking driver and ask to make a few pictures of him. More often than not, he would grin and toss off something like, "Knock yourself out." If he was grouchy or sullen or angry, chances are the next driver would remark, "Don't worry about him; he probably called home and his wife's boyfriend answered the phone." Their friendliness and humor dispersed my tension.

After driving all day in whatever weather or traffic presented itself, I would pull into a truck stop to have dinner before continuing to drive into the night or maybe to call it quits for the day. Worn out from the constant rumbling noise and vibration of the truck, I did not always feel like photographing. I just wanted to eat and take a long, hot shower, read a book and relax, keep to myself like everyone else was doing. But I had to override that desire: now it was time for me to go to work as a photographer. I felt compelled to photograph, to talk to people. I had to be "on," because as soon as my flash went off in the restaurant or truckers' lounge, I would be very visible. It was always more difficult to photograph inside a truck stop where my flash drew attention to myself and where I sometimes felt I was invading someone's private time. Outside, I wasn't confined by the space or concerned about my flash bouncing off the walls illuminating an often dimly lit space, and I could approach people a little more easily.

I was often struck by the wonders of travel and change—the country being slowly revealed to me as I drove across it, after a year or two covering every major highway and many secondary roads and every city. I formed a conceptual map of the nation and filled in the blanks as unknown regions became familiar. The cab of my truck became a cozy little cabin as I sat parked for the night at a truck stop somewhere or next to a warehouse waiting to unload the next morning. I felt especially snug and comfortable driving across New Mexico heading into a sunset or across western Montana with a full moon and no sign of life anywhere around except for an occasional light from a nearby town or isolated farmhouse or a scattering of cows lingering between patches of snow as bright as could be under a sky filled with stars. Sometimes there was just nothing like it: nearly eighty thousand pounds of truck and freight and some nice music on the radio and a cup of hot coffee from the last place I stopped—such serenity and peace. My head was clear and life was magnificent.

I even liked driving in New York. It was a thrill to load on the East Coast one weekend and deliver on the West Coast the next, crossing every state in between—forests, mountains, farms, and cities, six or seven hundred miles a day. There is a seductive side to trucking—the constant change, the anticipation of the unknown, the freedom of being removed from your context and set out into the world, the feeling you get when nobody knows where you are but you. You are only accountable to yourself and to your truck and transporting its contents safely across the country on time.

I was proud to be a truck driver and to be out on my own, working and challenging myself to enter new situations and learn from them, to solve the problems that arose: getting there on time, planning my trip, deciding how many miles to drive each day, making delivery appointments, maintaining and repairing my truck, calling road service to fix a flat or have my fuel pump rebuilt, helping other drivers slide their tandems to adjust their loads or loosen a frozen brake shoe, calling on the CB for directions to a shipper and having someone respond immediately with perfect instructions including details of landmarks and difficult maneuvers I would have to make. I learned to back up well and to drive safely, to pull straight into a parking spot sometimes instead of backing in so I could wake up and look into a field instead of a parking lot, and not to park by a reefer (a refrigerated trailer) because of the noise. I discovered that if I just sat behind the wheel all day I could get across the country in five days or so and then turn around and do it all over again.

The particulars of the life of long haul truck drivers create a connectedness, an unspoken bond among the truckers. The orange glow of cigarette ashes tossed from the truck ahead affirms that there is a person up there, doing the same thing you are, day after day—waiting for the end of a long stretch of driving to relax in a truckers' lounge, your surrogate living room, meant to be homelike and relaxing but most often cold and stark, alienating and discomforting. At most truck stops you can, however, count on a hot shower, a clean bathroom, and a fairly decent meal.

The romance of trucking is difficult to keep alive as extended days and nights behind the wheel add up to one long solitary journey. Everywhere you are is just anywhere but home. Everyone you meet is from somewhere else. And you will probably never see any of them again. You become accustomed to constant movement or maybe you never do, and you keep dreaming of a way to make things different.

The intensity, the gruelling physical strain, and the loneliness on the road induced a deep introspection I had not found elsewhere. There was so much time to let my mind wander, to explore my own emotions, to ponder an idea for days at a time virtually uninterrupted. On the road, my mind whirling with thoughts and images, palms sweating with anticipation, I was constantly analyzing my photographs and the life I wanted to live.

The roles of truck driver and photographer have been integral to my personal growth and to the formation and realization of my dreams. I do not know if I'll ever drive a truck again, but I can say with certainty that all I ever photograph will be enhanced by that experience.

Abilene, Texas 1994 ▶

Plymouth, Indiana 1988

The Big Engines
In the Night—
The Diesel on the Pass
—Jack Kerouac, "Mexico City Blues"

That's the Job by Bryan Di Salvatore

It can be mean out there on the American highway. Study these drivers' eyes. Not violent mean— not stick-a-gun-in-your-ribs, give-me-your-wallet mean. Things like that happen, but I'm talking about tired-making mean. Wear-you-down mean. Grind-you-to-dust mean.

Think of the last time you drove too far, peered down that road tunnel too long. How, when you got out of the car, the world seemed to rush in retreat because it had been charging you for so long. How your exhaustion mystified you—you'd been sitting all day long. How you couldn't sleep.

Go out the next morning and do it again. And the morning after that. For twenty, twenty-five days out of every month.

Study their eyes.

Look at them, sitting there on the pastel truck stop vinyl. Leaning on the formica, hands around red or gold plastic glasses, the ones with the golf-ball dimples, the ones that every truck stop in America seems to use. Look at the baskets of burgers and fries, chicken and fries. At the banks of phone booths; at the notices for loads and pay too good to be true. The posters of lost, missing, damaged children. The framed prints of sentimental art. The indoor-outdoor carpet. The linoleum. The too-thin towels and the too-small soap bars in the too-small showers. The signs for truck stop chapels; for AA meetings. The ping and donk and brrr and yuya of video games.

There they sit, far from home—always far from home: Renton, Washington; Richwood, Kentucky; Senatobia, Mississippi; Massena, New York; Torrance, California; Riverdale, Iowa; Tucumcari, New Mexico; Umatilla, Oregon; Vidalia, Louisiana; Exit 250; Exit 147; Exit 375; I-80; I-25; I-10; I-94—stirring their coffee, smoking their smokes, calling home. Where's home? Most likely in another area code.

Study their eyes. Even the young ones: red, sunk, lined, weary, always weary. Old. Even at their best—just out of a morning shower after a good night's sleep—drivers have that just-waked from a too-short nap look. Graveyard-shift eyes. Somewhere between vulnerable and wary, startled and resigned.

Study their arms, their shoulders, their posture—you don't build muscles sitting behind power steering; even in the best-designed seats, you begin to slump. Look at their paunch—spend a few years out there, even with the truck stops doing their best, offering salads and yoghurt and diet plates— you end up eating fried. Comfort food. And, unless you've got the willpower of a saint, there's no time for exercise, damnit; no place to run.

13

Interstate 10, Westbound, New Mexico 1994

Keep it between the lines, son. Keep the shiny side up, sister.

Roll, truck, roll. Ten, twelve, sixteen hours a day—I don't care what the law says, and most drivers don't either. Six, seven, eight days a week. If they hire on and drive someone else's truck, they earn two bits a mile, let's call it. If they drive their own truck—if they're owner operators—let's call it a dollar a mile.

Two bits a mile, a little more here, a little less there. Minus meals, minus lodging, minus those phone calls home. Say you're fresh; it's Kansas in May and your tanks are full: you might be good for six-hundred miles. King of the road.

But say it's Montana in February and you're heading west. Blowing a storm. Ice along the Yellowstone out of Billings. Chain up through Livingston Canyon at fifteen below—if they haven't closed the road. Take 'em off at the other end. Chain up to climb and drop Cardwell Hill. Take 'em off at Whitehall. Chain up for Homestake Pass. Take 'em off in Butte. Ice along the Clark Fork from Garrison Junction to St. Regis. Chain up for Lookout Pass. Unchain in Idaho. Chain up for Fourth of July Pass. Take 'em off outside Coeur d'Alene. Ground blizzards across the frozen wheatfields of eastern Washington. Chain up for Snoqualmie. Take 'em off east of Issaquah. By the time you get to Tacoma, it's Friday and too late to unload. Lay over until Monday. The boss don't pay you to park it.

Roll truck roll. Through North Dakota in January, with north winds butting broadside hard enough to push eighty-thousand pounds of tractor, trailer, load, and driver into the borrow pit.

Across the vacancy of Texas in August when you need gloves to uncap a fuel tank. Across Wyoming when it's cold enough to freeze flame.

Midsummer anywhere, and escadrilles of bugs slay themselves across the windshield like soldiers in a hopeless war.

South along I-95 in Florida; north along I-5 in Orange County. Disney World and Disneyland are only some words on exit signs.

West across Nebraska, into a satanic, sharpshooting sun drawing a laser bead on your optic nerves.

Tarping a load in Green Bay with a wind-chill of minus 8 and the canvas folds like cardboard.

Through West Virginia bottom fog, opaque as a shower curtain. Through the grease-slick ice-rain of Missouri. Through harvest-time dust thick enough to chew. The intestinal backroads of New England. The damnable Dallas traffic. The damnable Atlanta traffic. The damnable San Francisco traffic. The traffic. The traffic.

Watch out. Watch out.

Fueling in Aberdeen in December at 2 a.m. You're pumping fuel under the cathedral-high canopies at a truck stop and the acrid, revolting exhaust from your stacks drops to hound you like smoke from a heathen's campfire.

You're sick of your tapes and all you can find on the radio is country with too many violins or some showman who knows what's best for your soul.

Held over in Youngstown by balky injectors. In Ponca City, Oklahoma, with a busted hose. In Lansing with a short that has your headlights flicking

Sikeston, Missouri 1990

on-off like neon in the wrong part of town. Thirty miles east of Limon, Colorado, with a couple hundred thousand dollars of frozen fish in the trailer and a reefer unit that decides cold means hot. A hundred miles out of Yuma with a separated recap, the thick tongue of rubber thwapping loud as a cuckold on a motel-room door.

There's more: Jammed loading docks. Inept warehousemen. Permits. Bad directions to a construction project on a county road where you're to drop off a load of pipe. Tolls. Scalehouses. A state trooper who had a fight with his wife that morning. Mid-Wednesday and the delivery place is shut tight— it's a state holiday for someone you never heard of.

Lumbering RVs driven by carefree retirees. State highways built by the governor's brother-in-law. Rubberneckers in Oldsmobiles. Bolting deer. Dogs leaping for Frisbees. Drunk teenagers.

Study their eyes. They got that way bringing it to you: Parsley, kitty litter, barbeque grills, ballpoint pens, Ford Rangers, pantyhose, dictionaries, steel-belted radials, moccasins, fly rods, vodka, cigarette lighters, satellite dishes, ski poles. Contact lenses. Ben and Jerry's. The rebar that braces your dwelling, the shingles that cover your head, the windows in your den, the sheet metal on the signs on the roads you drive, the gasoline you put in your car to get you down that road, the resin that becomes the plastic that houses the cassettes you play as you drive, the parts for the tractors that plow the fields in which grow the crops that become the food you eat. Leotards. Golf carts. Pigs, live; chickens, frozen. Mattresses, coffins, wristwatches, mobile homes, combines, wheat, sulfur, sausages, lumber, Hush Puppies, cop-

ing saws, hamburger buns. The paper that becomes this page you hold, the ink for this comma, the glue that binds this book. Baseball bats and baseball caps. Beer cups and peanut sacks. Mighty Morphin Power Rangers. Laptops. Floppy disks.

What you need, what you want.

Not too many years ago, doing research, I spent a good portion of the late summer and early fall riding around this crumpled, sprawling, favored land of ours up in the cab of a big ol' truck. It was red; it was a conventional (with the engine out in front—as opposed to a cabover, where the cab is above the engine), and it was driven by a fellow I hadn't met before who turned out to be one of my favorite people in the world—Lonnie Umphlett.

Lonnie is one of those walking contradictions. A born-and-raised southerner who lives in western Montana; a clean-living and gentle soul whose full beard and long hair suggest he might be on loan from the Gypsy Jokers; a devout, fundamentalist Christian with the wickedly rueful sense of humor of a pagan; a devoted family man who, because of his job, lives three-quarters of his life far from the hearth; an agrarian-at-heart who spends most of his time in the clang and bustle of industrial, commercial America.

Sometimes, when we were out in the middle of nowhere, I camped in my sleeping bag under the truck trailer; sometimes, when we found ourselves in sketchy, urban areas, Lonnie generously invited me to bunk with him in the sleeper attached to his truck cab. Sometimes, when we had to lay over for a couple of days, I popped for a motel.

Bordentown, New Jersey 1988

We were a Laurel and Hardy odd pair. Lonnie, blond and slight and wound tight as an eight-dollar watch; me, dark and wide and flabby and tending toward the lethargic; Lonnie tobacco-free and a virtual tee-totaler; me a smoker who cares for a six-pack; Lonnie devoted to the Chicago Bears, me convinced there are no other sports than baseball; Lonnie a devotee of sermons and Bob Seeger on the tape deck, me of Merle, The Stones, and Van Morrison; Lonnie, as I've said, a sincere Christian, me a practicing agnostic; Lonnie a profound sleeper; me a thrash-and-snort buffalo boy.

All in all we made a good team. Had a lot of laughs, solved most of the world's immediate problems. He taught me how to help him tarp loads. Lonnie's trailer was a flatbed. While I was with him he hauled 2 x 4s and 2 x 10s, some sort of weird panelling stuff, twenty-thousand pound steel coils, iron grinding balls for a phosphate mine, 8-inch PVC pipe, scaffolding, and more steel coils. I took care of some rudimentary pathfinding. I got us down the road most of the time, but once, to my profound embarrassment, I convinced Lonnie to try "this blue line here. It looks like a straight shot." It was not. It was a twisty, up-and-down, twenty-five mile-an-hour nightmare—what Lonnie called a "five-thousand shift road." Lonnie, bless his frugal soul, usually had to be dragged kicking and screaming into accepting my occasional offers to treat us to a room. Whenever he put up a fuss, I drew my ace in the hole: I owed him, big time, for having blithely sent us—hungry and tired—down that ridiculous, intestinal Utah highway.

We traveled all over the damn place: Montana to Minneapolis to Green Bay to Milwaukee to Chicago to Lodi, New Jersey, to Pittsburgh to St. Louis to Kansas City to Denver to Aberdeen, South Dakota, to Youngstown and Columbus, Ohio, to Vernal, Utah, to Denver to Salt Lake City to Las Vegas to Kansas City to Los Angeles. Once, we thought the dispatcher was going to send us to Savannah. I joked with Lonnie that I didn't have a visa. He said isn't that just like a damn Yankee. We ran into everything but ice and snow: cat-and-dog rain, panther-and-wolf rain, hail, wind, fog, blinding sun, dust, smog, and traffic jams bad enough to make you weep or want to. We saw a couple of terrible accidents. Once, we passed some firemen dousing a horse trailer on the side of I-71 in Ohio. A bit farther on, we saw a man with a rifle standing next to a horse whose mane was still burning. We listened to football games—pro, college and high school—on the radio. We watched preposterous movies on the motel premium channels. We drove behind idiots. We saw prostitutes working truck stop parking lots. We smelled marijuana smoke. Once a driver we didn't know offered us some pepper-uppers over the CB on Interstate 80. We saw some almighty sunsets and a couple of metro skylines so magnificent from a few miles off they made us believe in a better future.

Besides helping navigate and tarp, I took on some chores. I fueled us up; checked fluids (then asked Lonnie to double-check them); saw to the windshields, side-windows and mirrors; bumped tires (then asked Lonnie to bump them again), and entertained Lonnie—got him howling with laughter or outrage—by reading him selected stories from the newspapers I bought along the way.

Lonnie would say things like, "I was near Buffalo and had to run down to Atlanta" or "Once I was running from Seattle to Dallas." This is how drivers talk. It is, for me, the best indicator of how many miles they drive. A trip across three states, for them, is the same as a trip across three counties is for the rest of us.

He could tell, within an hour—and barring something out of the ordinary happening—when we would arrive at a place eight hundred miles away. If I quizzed him (Lonnie is a very tolerant guy) and said: "How far is it from New Orleans to Boise?" he'd come up with an answer that did Rand-McNally proud. Once, as we were heading out of a truck stop, I put my hand over Lonnie's tachometer. As he climbed through the gears, I would ask him how many RPMs he was at. He hit, as I recall, ten out of twelve numbers on the nose and the other two on the chin.

I figured Lonnie was a savant, but he told me that any good driver, one who had many hundreds of thousands of miles under his belt, could probably do the same thing. "I'm different, but I'm not unusual" was how he put it. "You have to know your turf out here. Just like DiMaggio knew the ballparks, like Nicklaus knows the greens."

Besides amazement, and besides the answers to a lot of "What's that for?" questions, Lonnie provided me something much more abstract, much less trivial. He opened a door for me—his overstaying guest in that tiny, mobile apartment of his—on an elusive, profoundly misunderstood world.

When, on a fine summer afternoon, I first climbed into Lonnie's Freight-liner, I did so with a vision of truck driving flush with romanticism. It was also, as I found out, a common and threadbare vision: the long-distance driver as The Last American Cowboy.

The phrase was coined as paean. It meant to conjure youth, vitality, competence, independence. The driver/cowboy of this vision is male. He is white. There he stands, briefly; there he goes, quickly, anywhere he wishes, anytime he wants. His continent is a patch and he knows its every bush and rise and draw. He is tall, sinewy, slim-hipped, wide-shouldered. Capable. Slow to anger, fast to draw. What he knows like the back of his hand, we—mere amateurs, sedan and station-wagon people, sedentary burghers—can only guess at.

Drivers, in my mind, were, to a one, polite, gentle, tough, compassionate, wise in practical things. If gruff, they had good reason to be so. They were beholden to no man. They laid their head at night wherever they found themselves. They left us in their dust, these drivers, moving—as Jack Kerouac wrote in *Visions of Cody*—"beyond the whatevers of where you who watch them still stay. . .yonder never to come back again."

Well, yes.

But, as others have pointed out, and as I learned, that conjured cowboy is the fictive cowboy, the mythological cowboy, the dime-novel cowboy—Gary Cooper in "The Virginian," perhaps. The historical, actual cowboy was something else.

Some cowboys were black; many were Mexican; a few, at least, were women; cowboys had to work in all weather; cowboys had to work

Burley, Idaho 1989

Richwood, Kentucky 1994

intolerably long hours; cowboy wages were meager at best, even though cowboys were responsible for enormously valuable property; cowboys spent the majority of their time away from home; cowboys worked, more often than not, for owners who lived in comfort far from the dust of the trail; cowboy work was dangerous; cowboy work was tedious; cowboy work was repetitive; cowboy work was difficult; cowboy work demanded great skill; cowboys were invisible most of the time, and not especially welcome in town. Polite society needed, wanted, the fruit of cowboy labor, but polite society neither needed, nor wanted, to brush actual shoulders with the cowboy himself. Very few cowboys got rich. They aged quickly. Mothers didn't want their daughters to marry one.

By the time I climbed out of Lonnie's cab in Studio City, California—on a hot, smoggy November Thursday with the sky yellow as disease—I was no longer a schoolboy romantic. I realized that I hadn't known the first thing that went on up there in those monstrous machines I had seen on the road all my life.

We chatted for a few minutes on that California sidewalk, next to the muddy, dusty truck. Idling across from a fancy restaurant and in front of the manicured entrance to a television-and-movie production office, the rig looked out of place—like some mutt looking for a meal at the pedigree club. I called it a long-haul Mercedes. Lonnie made a joke about getting a ticket for misdemeanor lowering of property values.

I wanted to go home, to my wife, my friends. I wanted to sleep in my own bed. I wanted to get some daily exercise, uncreak my bones. I wanted to eat homecooked food, at a table that wasn't illuminated by fluorescence. In short, I was tired of the road, of all that moving.

So was Lonnie.

But I was the one with the plane ticket home. He had a hot load of lumber waiting near San Rafael that needed to be in New York State. Maybe he'd be home for Thanksgiving.

"Well, did you learn something out here?" Lonnie asked just before he climbed back into the cab.

"Yeah, I think so. Some. I hope."

He swept his hand east, toward the continent and its two-hundred-odd million people. "They think . . . we're a bunch of knuckle-walkers and bullies, loaded up on potions and powder." He laughed. "That's not the half of it, not the quarter."

You get five or six miles to a gallon of fuel. When you fill up empty tanks, you better have enough money to pay for a couple of hundred gallons. When you change oil in a Freightliner or Mack or Kenworth or Peterbilt or a big GMC or Ford, you change eleven gallons of it. Climb the ladder from the lowest crawler gear to high overdrive, you'll shift ten, or thirteen or fifteen or eighteen times. Lonnie once estimated that, in one six-hundred mile stretch of turnpike driving, he had to shift one hundred and sixty-two times just approaching and leaving toll booths and scalehouses.

A high-end new truck—I'm talking about the business end, commonly called the tractor, which includes the cab, the sleeping compartment, the engine, the two driving axles, the front axle, and ten tires—will run you, pretty easy, one hundred thousand dollars and change. Lettering extra. With good luck, regular maintenance, and a watchful eye, you might put two-thirds of a million miles on a new truck without replacing much more than oil, filters, and tires.

A truck engine is about four feet high, five feet long, and just shy of a yard wide. It approaches five-hundred horsepower. It generates twelve hundred foot-pounds of torque—about four times that of a full-size pick-up truck. If you're not careful when you shift low gears, all that power will lift the front left fender easy as a diner tipping a soup bowl.

Everything is oversized. The steering wheel is bigger than a jumbo pizza; the tires near tall as a Honda Civic; the gear-shift has the girth of a walking stick; the mirrors are wide and long as dachshunds; the windshield the size of a sliding glass door—once, after a long trip with Lonnie, I got briefly, seriously, claustrophobic driving home in my Ford: it was like looking out a motel room peep-eye.

Trucks are workplaces. I happen to think that trucks are handsome vehicles—the image that keeps coming to mind whenever I see one heading down the road is of a bull elk in full stride. But, first and foremost, they are functional, overtly so.

Take a look: fenders jut from the hood like sprung barrel staves; turn signals jut from fenders like mouse ears; they bristle with mirrors and antennae, air horns, lug nuts, fuel tanks, exhaust pipes, battery cases, a spare tire or two under the trailer, snow chains, storage boxes. With its H-beams, riv-

ets and, in older trucks, the air filters, large as milk pails, all exposed, a truck is like a pair of trousers turned inside out on a clothesline, every seam and stitch facing the sun.

You step into a car; you scale a truck. A cab floor is four feet above ground level; you climb on metal running boards, and hoist yourself with the help of any of several chrome handles into the seat. Riding in a truck cab is eerie. You don't hug the road so much as perch above it. The familiar swath of pavement seen from a sedan becomes, from a truck cab, a dark beam, narrow as a monorail. Other vehicles mutate, too, from that conning tower perspective—instead of banks of metal and glass encasing disembodied heads, they become sociological dioramas: a pair of cautious oldsters surrounded by maps, boxes of tissues, thermos bottles; sportsmen with creels, rifles, camp stoves, waders; college students with computers, cardboard boxes of books; salesmen with sample cases. And, yes, knees and thighs exposed by hiked-up skirts. I kept hearing, from various drivers, the same story. It concerns a woman driver, either naked, or wearing only a blouse, who positions her car alongside a truck for miles and miles, allowing the driver an arresting view. I asked Lonnie about this. He sighed, then laughed, then sighed again. "Two things," he said. "One, the only way you get that view is if she's riding shotgun. Two, this is a lonely job and you have a lot of time to let your mind run wild. Drivers have a real problem with boredom."

Eventually, riding in a truck seems normal. At first, however, it resembles riding in a car like being a jockey resembles going to the track. Cars are designed to obscure reality, just as passenger jets are. Ideally, a plane has the

Columbus, Mississippi 1989

Interstate 80, Eastbound, Iowa 1989

feel of a living room—the less sound the better; the less turbulence the better. Ideally, a car should be a floating carpet—forgiving springs, silence, no sense that you are being moved down the road by exploding fuel, racing pistons, meshing gear teeth.

It just isn't that easy to cloud reality in a truck. Noise is there, and it isn't white. The engine, though invisible, is omnipresent—a rough baritone, the growling of a hundred jungle cats. You can *feel* the thing, though there's competition. Trucks don't roll so much as lurch, and bounce, and shake—the trailer is a very temperamental passenger, either balky and pouting, impatient and whiny. Mirrors shake themselves out of position; a ballpoint pen on the dash will soon enough bounce itself to the floor; the surface of a cup of coffee is a welter of ripples. Like on a boat, everything needs to be stowed, and nothing stays stowed forever. Lonnie kept a few cardboard supply boxes in his sleeper, filled with food treats and extra clothes. No matter how well he bungee-corded them, or how tightly he wedged them together, sooner or later they made their entrance into the cab. He dubbed them "The Things That Took Over The Freightliner."

And all this fuss I'm talking about takes place in a loaded truck, whose howitzer-barrel shocks and brick-thick springs are designed for loads. An empty truck along a patchy highway is an aluminum skiff bolting across a tricorn sea.

That said, however, the cab of a modern truck is an extremely cool place to be. You feel important. Cab isn't the right word—cockpit is better—all that's lacking is a flight attendant serving coffee and supper. Even with the increased noise level, and the jostly ride, a modern truck cab is ergonomically superior—hands down—to the most outrageously expensive passenger car. There's a simple reason for that—it is the rare passenger car that needs to sustain for its driver the intricate balance between comfort and alertness, for so many hours at a stretch, that a truck must.

The seats have lots of leg room. They are high-backed and stiff enough to keep your attention. They are air-powered, allowing for an infinite number of adjustments. (Sometimes I'd get bored and lower the seat so that only the bill of my baseball cap was visible out the side window. I thought this was pretty funny, but sooner or later Lonnie would get embarrassed. "I can't take you anywhere," he'd say.) The clutch is stiff—like pushing a box of books across the floor; the fuel pedal is goosey and the brake powerful—overstep it and a truck will lock up like a bad knee. The dash roughly follows the bend of the steering wheel—like an amphitheater—and the array of gauges (sixteen of them in Lonnie's truck, measuring everything from RPMs and MPH to air pressure and rear axle temperature) and toggle switches (mostly for lights, but also for things like defrosting side mirrors or adjusting them) and dials and buttons, fascinated me like photos of command modules did in my youth.

In the daytime, running down the road in the cab of a truck is like having the best seat in the house—on the occasions we drove down highways I was familiar with, I kept blurting to Lonnie things like "Look at that!" and "So *that's* what's over that rise!" and "Hey, that ranch has a swimming pool!"

At night, it can be downright cozy—once, Lonnie and I were heading across the Poconos toward Harrisburg. It was cool, just-south-of-comfort-able outside, drizzling and murky. A breeze threw early-falling leaves across the road. The woods—what I could see of them, looked dense and forbid-ding. And there we were, high, dry and warm, flying along, chatting about this and that, with an uninterrupted medley of Beatles songs coming through the radio from somewhere far away. The red dome light, and the soft amber glow from the dash made it seem as if we were sitting by a small fireplace in a cabin in the north woods.

But I'm not a driver. Somewhere near Kansas City, as we headed into traffic and I said to Lonnie, for about the seven-hundredth time, "Jeez, the view is really something from up here" (Did I mention that Lonnie was a very tolerant fellow?), he gave me a lesson.

"I 'preciate the view. I do. It makes my life out here tolerable. But what else do you see besides centerfield over there?" (We had just passed the Kansas City Royals' ballpark.)

I said something like, "I don't know. Stuff."

"I see a line of cars up the road. I'm concentrating on the eighth car ahead. And the sixth car. And the fifth and the third and the rest. I'm lookin' at 'em all. The car just ahead, that's important, 'cause it's the one that's gonna get squarshed underneath this bad boy if something happens, but there's only so much I can do about that. But if I look a few cars ahead . . ."

"Gotcha. Lonnie, is this just your way of driving or . . .?"

"Nope. Every driver alive. Or darn near. That's the job, see, that's the job."

I felt, rightly, abashed. All those miles—I had come to think of myself as

an old hand—and, plain as day, I was still driving my Falcon. A truck driver keeps one foot in the present and the other in the future. Not just four or five cars in the future, but four or five hours, even, at times, four or five states, and occasionally, four or five days.

"Look," Lonnie told me, "Damn near any fool can point this thing down the road. The trick comes in anticipating."

Knowing what you have to do today to get somewhere on time tomor-row or the next day. The driver wants to make money and not sit around, and the boss wants to make money, and the customer wants that load so he can make money. It's the American way.

So a driver—a good driver—has to know his own habits and limitations, and find out about the habits and limitations of everyone else in America. If he knows he tends to sleep seven hours, and he knows he wakes up, nor-mally, around six in the morning, he might push hard for a couple of days so that on that third day he wakes within a shout of his unloading place, so he can be there when it opens.

An hour lost here, an hour lost there, and a driver finds himself at the unloading spot at lunch hour. There's another hour. Or he finds himself at the unloading spot at closing time. There's a bag of hours. He has to call ahead—some places only accept loads on certain days, at certain times. Every time a driver pulls off the highway, it takes time—Lonnie figures a half-hour or forty-five minutes no matter what he needs to do—so he combines eating with fueling and goes to fuel at places that are easy to get to (most of them are) and efficient (a lot of places aren't).

Customers generally work a five-day, forty-hour week. Drivers don't. If

Wheat Ridge, Colorado 1990

Indianapolis, Indiana 1994

drivers are clever, they have the drop on the customer. If they aren't, they twiddle their thumbs a lot. If a truck is heading into a big city—Los Angeles, say—to unload on a Monday, he might be smart to top off the tanks in Las Vegas, or even Salt Lake, and push all the way to the customer—right to the loading dock if he can—on a Sunday night. That's because, as Lonnie told me, " 'bout every truck in the country is heading into L.A. it seems, and the truck stops are jammed all the way to the Arizona border, so don't even *think* about finding a place to park if you're coming in late."

And don't even *think* about wrestling with the commuter traffic. And, if you're in downtown or a lot of places in major cities, fueling places might be scarce or difficult to find. The trick is to get in early if you can, unload, find where you're going next, and get started there.

Without having to run around looking for fuel, and before the afternoon traffic begins and the freeways set up.

Any fool. . . . It takes skill to do it with grace.

I had, before I went on the road, assumed there was always room at truck stops, as if their huge lots expanded with each arrival, some tractor-trailer version of the miracle of the loaves and fish. As well, I had in my mind some Norman Rockwell vision of what a truck stop was: a little cafe verging on a wildflower-thick, high-green field. The cafe was painted red and white and had gingham curtains and the best homemade pies you ever ate. The kitchen was run by a plump, grandmotherly woman. There were three waitresses—Rhonda, Babs, and Mary Lou. Rhonda was a sultry redhead with

enough ex-husbands to field a basketball team; Babs smoked too much, knew every joke on earth, and could swear like a trooper. She had the drivers' respect. Flirting was fine, but everyone knew she had a sickly husband at home. Mary Lou was sad-eyed, quiet, and pretty as the day is long. One day she'd meet the right man—a handsome, hard-working driver named Joe—and they'd buy a farm and raise a family.

I may have mentioned this to Lonnie once. He may have looked at me and said "Lord have mercy."

In fact, truck stops are as various in personality as are American communities: some are urban and low-down gone-wrong, some are, in fact, cheery and rural. Most of them, these days, are large chain operations that offer, for better or worse, familiarity. They are, in fact, less like gas stations than they are communities themselves—even to the point of having their own security cops. At night, they become weird dormitories—their lots packed with dozens, and, in many cases, hundreds, of idling or silent trucks, some with curtains around their glass, some with the soft light of a television filtering through, some with signs warning off the denizens of the night that sometimes frequent these places: "No whores," "No drugs." Most long-haul trucks have sleeping units attached to the cab. Some have single beds, some have double beds. Some you can stand in, some you crawl into. Some have room for a small refrigerator, some have room for a small television. Some have an upstairs. Some have climate control. Some are nicer than places I've lived.

Fuel and food and truck-washing and repair services are the bare

Wise, North Carolina 1989

minimum of modern truck stop offerings. Most have shower rooms. Many have adjoining motels and lounges. There is almost always a shop of some sort, offering, at convenience-store prices, a variety of necessities and non-necessities: maps, atlases, sunglasses, watches, CBs, TVs, knives, antennas, snack food, fruit, toiletries and over-the-counter medicines, cowboy boots, gloves, pants, shirts, baseball caps, truck accessories (chrome-plated lug nuts, seat covers, air fresheners), quick gifts for wives and children and sweethearts, coolers, music tapes and audio tapes. Books on tape, one clerk told me, just fly off the shelves. Drivers rent them, and return them by mail or in person to affiliated truck stops. I like the idea of drivers, thousands of them, running down the road, listening to L'Amour and Grisham and Anne Rice and maybe John Le Carre. In one truck stop I saw an unabridged tape of Joyce's *Dubliners* and an unabridged *Frankenstein*.

Drivers can get their hair cut and their shoes shined; they can dink around in a video arcade, cash checks, send off paperwork via the mail or private shipping companies, go to chapel, renew a driver's license, do their laundry, wire flowers. They can behave badly if they wish. Some do. Most don't.

But, finally, what even the best truck stops can't offer is much more than a faint—sincere, but faint—simulacrum of home. The temporary citizens of truck stops are not family, they are not even friends. The encounters are brief and familiar and, often as not, pro forma.

"I tell a joke to a waitress," Lonnie told me, "just to talk to another human being, and she may laugh, but she's got twenty orders to fill, and she's probably heard the joke before."

The saddest moments I had out there on the road occurred in truck stops. I overheard one poor guy on the phone saying "I give you all the goddamn money I have, and most of what I haven't even seen yet. I'm out here in damn Minnesota busting ass and all you can do is sit there and complain." He looked closer to tears than to homicide.

Oh, the open road! More than permanent transience, more than constant anonymity, the defining aspect of the job of the American truck driver is loneliness. Separation.

A little spat before the driver heads off for two weeks. An evening call home, a hope for a little sweet talk, and the kids are acting up, and the washing machine has overflowed. The bills are due and the television is showing reruns all around.

Think of the missed opportunities: parent-teacher night; a date at the movies; a barbeque with friends in the back yard; church on Sunday; a half-hour of laughs with "Seinfeld." Think of the burden of the left-at-home: one less errand-runner; one less homework-helper; one less disciplinarian; one less home repairer; one less bolsterer. Day after day; week after week.

Lonnie puts it this way: "You talk about something, I don't care what, one of those husband-and-wife things that need talking about. Maybe there's a hasty word, a tired word, one of those words you regret soon as it leaves your mouth. And then you run down the road for a few hundred miles, dwelling on this, dwelling on that. After a while, the little whatever-it-was begins chipping at the rock, past the enamel to the sensitive stuff."

I still love to watch the trucks roll by, admire their paint jobs, their nicknames, their customized lighting schemes; I like listening to their deep roar on a clear summer night as they catch gears, heading up a grade. I wonder where they're bound, what they're hauling, what they've seen, what they'll see next. I read the sides of truck cabs, and imagine what they're like, those strange and soaring American place names: Black Eagle, Iola, Ulysses, John Day, Sparkman, Crooked Oak, ten thousand more.

But . . .

But . . .

A while back, my wife and I were eating a late breakfast in Sheridan, Wyoming. A truck from south Florida—it was a boat hauler, empty—pulled out slowly from the lot across from the cafe.

It was the day before Christmas Eve.

My wife asked if the driver would be home for Christmas.

I thought about it, did some rough figuring, and shook my head no. "Unless he knows a hell of a shortcut."

We made it home—we'd been many states away for several months—and our Christmas was merry. There were shrieking nephews and nieces and grandpas and grandmas and friends and neighbors. Aunts and uncles, and a roaring fire and Christmas carols and a bit too much wine. I walked outside for some air and thought about that Florida driver. Where was he? Oklahoma? Arkansas? Illinois? I didn't know, except it wasn't home.

"Honey," I imagined him saying on the phone from somewhere, "You go ahead. Hold back some presents, we'll celebrate Monday, Tuesday at the latest. Tell the kids . . ."

Tell 'em what? Tell 'em what?

Give 'em a little room, the men and women driving those trucks. Don't believe but one in fifty the stories you hear about the drugs and the drunks and the partying—no matter how well-paid and smart-haired the source.

Study their eyes.

It's a job of work. A hard job of work. Remember that.

Raymond, Mississippi 1988

El Paso, Texas 1988

Bourbon, Indiana 1990 ▶

Sayre, Oklahoma 1988

◀ WaKeeney, Kansas 1990

Salt Lake City, Utah 1988

Sinclair, Wyoming 1988

Bristol, Tennessee 1988

Houston, Texas 1989

Holladay, Tennessee 1994

Bristol, Tennessee 1994 ▶

Midway, Missouri 1989

Breezewood, Pennsylvania 1994

Evansville, Indiana 1989

Saluda, North Carolina 1994

Cottondale, Alabama 1994

Tallapoosa, Georgia 1989

Walcott, Iowa 1990

Senatobia, Mississippi 1994

Carlisle, Pennsylvania 1988

Des Moines, Iowa 1989

Buckhorn, Pennsylvania 1990

Amarillo, Texas 1989

Dillon, South Carolina 1989 ▶

McDonough, Georgia 1987

Barkeyville, Pennsylvania 1990

Sikeston, Missouri 1990

North Bend, Washington 1994

Cottondale, Alabama 1988 ▶

Atlanta, Georgia 1994

Holbrook, Arizona 1994

Ontario, California 1988

Sonora, Kentucky 1989 ▶

Walcott, Iowa 1990

Boise, Idaho 1990

◀ Raphine, Virginia 1994

Denison, Texas 1994

Holbrook, Arizona 1994

Interstate 75, Southbound, Kentucky 1994 ▶

Laredo, Texas 1994

Manhattan Bridge, New York 1994

◀ Holbrook, Arizona 1994

Dunn, North Carolina 1994

Triadelphia, West Virginia 1994

Laredo, Texas 1994

Atlanta, Georgia 1994 ▶

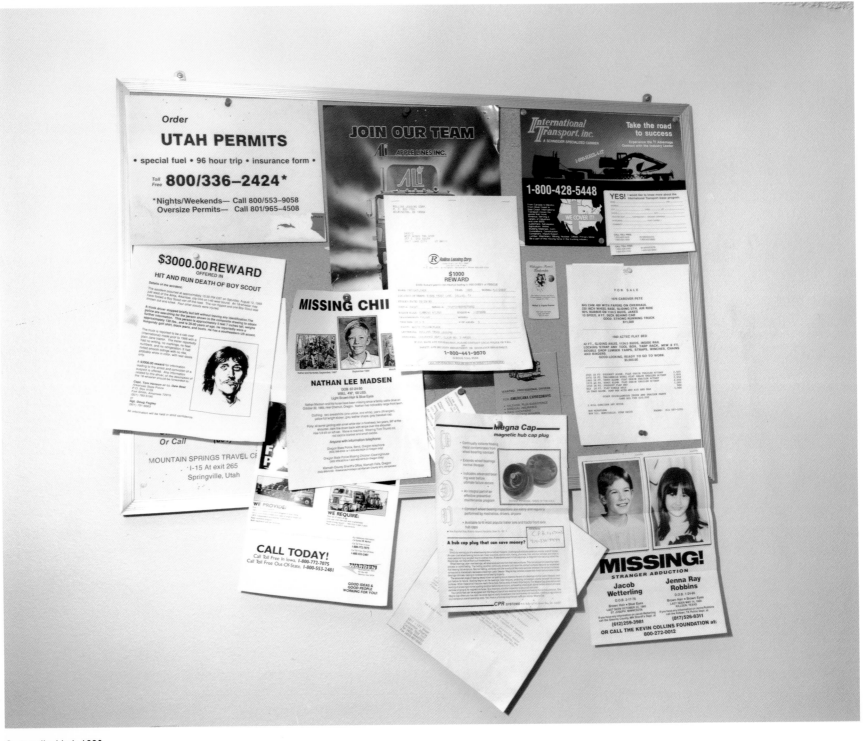

Springville, Utah 1990

Hubbard, Ohio 1990

Sayre, Oklahoma 1988

Acknowledgments

Thanks to many people for helping with this project:

My parents for giving me spirit and teaching me to see the big picture and for years of support and encouragement.

My sister, Karleen, who is always there.

My friends who believed in me and helped in many ways. Your friendship means a whole lot.

My teachers at the Rhode Island School of Design.

The John Simon Guggenheim Memorial Foundation and the curators that collected my work. Your support gave me confidence to keep working harder and to remain true to my own vision.

JoAnne Prichard at University Press of Mississippi for being able to see that box of photographs as a book and for her personal interest in the project.

John Langston for his thoughtful and sophisticated design of the book.

Bryan Di Salvatore for his excellent essay that puts the right words to the truckers' experience.

Ned Gray for making the final prints for the book.

The truck drivers for allowing me to photograph them and for sharing their lives with me.

And to Jane, I look forward to life with you. Maybe some of it will be on the road.